Marian Cox

Cambridge Checkpoint

English

Workbook

7

CAMBRIDGE
UNIVERSITY PRESS

CAMBRIDGE UNIVERSITY PRESS
Cambridge, New York, Melbourne, Madrid, Cape Town,
Singapore, São Paulo, Delhi, Mexico City

Cambridge University Press
The Edinburgh Building, Cambridge CB2 8RU, UK

www.cambridge.org
Information on this title: www.cambridge.org/9781107647817

First published 2012

Printed and bound in the United Kingdom by the MPG Books Group

A catalogue record for this publication is available from the British Library

ISBN 978-1-107-64781-7 Paperback

Contents

Introduction

Welcome to Cambridge Checkpoint English Stage 7.

The Cambridge Checkpoint English course covers the Cambridge Secondary 1 English framework and is divided into three stages: 7, 8 and 9.

This Workbook has 12 units which offer support in the skills covered in the corresponding units of the Stage 7 Coursebook. The topics in the Workbook are linked to the topics in the Coursebook.

There are two more workbooks in the series to cover stages 8 and 9, and these provide practice for progressive skills to match the skills covered in the corresponding coursebooks.

The Workbook exercises give extra practice in specific areas for students working alone or for students who need to develop a particular and relevant language skill or task approach.

The rules and key points introduced in the Coursebook are reinforced in the corresponding units of the Workbook, to make sure they have been fully understood and applied before students progress to the next unit.

The Workbook can be used as a differentiation resource for classroom work and for setting homework. The responses can be written in the spaces beneath the exercises. The introduction to each unit indicates the types of exercise it includes.

The answers to the Workbook exercises are on the Teacher Resource CD, which contains further relevant tasks, worksheets and handouts to support each of the Coursebook and Workbook units.

UNIT 1 House and home

This unit gives you practice in giving directions and instructions; defining and explaining; paraphrasing; recognising parts of speech; using full stops; double-letter spellings; forming similes; and skimming and scanning.

1 **Give clear, concise directions for how to get to the following places.**

a From your house to a friend's house.

Turn left at the gate . . .

....

....

....

....

....

b From a friend's house to your house.

....

....

....

....

....

....

c From your house to the nearest shopping centre.

....

....

....

....

....

....

2 **Give clear, concise instructions, in sentences, for how to do the following.**

a Pack a suitcase.

....

....

....

....

....

....

....

b Wrap a present.

....

....

....

....

....

....

c Boil an egg.

....

....

....

....

....

3 Write a letter or email to a relative, thanking them for giving you the money
to buy a present for your birthday or name day. Describe what you have bought,
and tell them how it will be useful or enjoyable.

....

....

....

....

....

....

....

....

....

....

....

....

....

4 **Think about the meaning of the proverbs and try to explain them by paraphrasing (changing them into your own words).**

a People who live in glass houses shouldn't throw stones.

....

....

....

b The grass is always greener on the other side of the fence.

....

....

....

c If you can't stand the heat, get out of the kitchen.

....

....

....

d Darkness reigns at the foot of the lighthouse.

....

....

....

e Good fences make good neighbours.

....

....

....

5a **Define each part of speech, then give five examples of each.**

Nouns: ....

....

Verbs: ....

....

Adjectives: ....

....

Adverbs: ....

....

Prepositions: ....

....

5b **What part of speech are the words below?**

a remember ....

b different ....

c teacher ....

d it ....

e frantically ....

f between ....

6 Put full stops and capital letters in the right places in the passage below. (Where there is no joining word, a full stop is needed.)

About this time I had an experience that taught me that nature is not always kind one day my teacher and I were returning from a long ramble the morning had been fine but it was growing warm and sultry when at last we turned our faces homeward two or three times we stopped to rest under a tree by the wayside our last halt was under a wild cherry tree a short distance from the house the shade was welcome and the tree was so easy to climb that with my teacher's assistance I was able to scramble to a seat in the branches it was so cool up in the tree that Miss Sullivan proposed that we have our luncheon there I promised to keep still while she went to the house to fetch it.

From The Story of My Life *by Helen Keller*

7 The spelling rule is that a long vowel is usually followed by a single consonant; a short vowel by a double consonant. Add 'ing' to these 20 verbs.

fill .... file ....

pine .... pin ....

hop .... hope ....

begin .... define ....

put .... pat ....

run .... come ....

ban .... forget ....

stare .... star ....

greet .... write ....

dine .... sit ....

8 **Complete the five similes using a comparison of your own.**

They leapt through the air .... *like monkeys.* ....

a The abandoned house was as scary as ....

....

b I was so relieved to arrive home that I felt as if ....

....

c The kids shouting in the school playground sounded like ....

....

d The teacher looked so angry that she reminded them of ....

....

e The feeling of being lost in the overgrown garden was similar to ....

....

9 **After you have skimmed the passage on page 8 for the gist (general meaning):**

a Write one sentence saying what its main points are.

....

....

....

....

....

Cambridge Checkpoint English 7

b Scan the passage and highlight or underline the signs that a house may be haunted.

People more often claim to have heard ghosts than to have seen them. Slamming doors, moving furniture and breaking glass are the most common sounds heard in so-called haunted houses, as well as the sound of footsteps, of course. The sound of objects flying around a room and crashing into things is also reported where a poltergeist is apparently involved. Musical instruments – pianos and violins especially – sometimes play themselves. Of the actual human noises, weeping and screaming are favourites. Ghosts rarely speak, it seems. When a spectral figure actually appears in person, it is nearly always wearing period costume of a sombre colour, or the long, shapeless, floating white garment which is traditional attire for ghosts. They are sometimes accompanied by transparent domestic animals, in particular dogs, cats and horses. Smells are also often mentioned by those who believe their house has a ghostly presence. Of these, the scent of flowers, especially roses, is the most common for some reason.

UNIT 2 Tall tales

This unit gives you practice in using parts of speech; speech verbs and speech punctuation; full stops; single dashes; compound sentences; and writing concisely.

1 Here are ten verbs to change into their noun forms, for example 'fail' → 'failure'. Most of them are irregular, so be careful.

lend   ....   seize   ....

spend   ....   catch   ....

do   ....   widen   ....

believe   ....   perceive   ....

interrupt   ....   agree   ....

2a Put inverted commas (speech marks) in the correct places in the passage below.

Saffia entered the house and put down her school bag. Her mother greeted her and asked How was your day?

Saffia answered with a cheeky smile. It was all right, although the elephant was a bit of a surprise.

What do you mean, the elephant? queried her astonished mother.

We were halfway through the biology lesson when an elephant wandered into our classroom.

Her mother didn't know whether her daughter was joking or not. She ventured to say That must have been fun.

Saffia went over to the fridge and opened it. I was enjoying it, until it ate my lunch. So I'm really hungry. I could eat an elephant.

2b Put full stops, capital letters and inverted commas (quotation marks) where necessary in the passage below.

An elderly couple who rarely went out received in the post a letter saying you have won a prize in a competition enclosed are free tickets to the theatre this Saturday they did not remember entering any competition and didn't particularly enjoy the theatre but they thought it would be a waste not to use the tickets so they went the theatre was quite a distance so they were away for many hours when they returned home they found the front door open and a message pinned to it which read hope you enjoyed the play on entering the house they discovered that it was completely empty all their possessions had been stolen

3 Put appropriate and different speech verbs, not including 'said', into the ten gaps below.

a 'Leave me alone!' she ....

b 'Finish your work quietly,' .... the teacher.

c As the children tiptoed through the house at night, one of them

.... , 'Shh! Nobody must hear us.'

d The postman .... , 'Get this dog off me!'

e At the other end of the phone a voice could be heard to

.... , 'I am closer than you think.'

f The headteacher .... , 'There will be a parents'

evening next Thursday for Year 7.'

g 'Sorry but I can't help you with your homework. I'm not very good at English,'

.... his father.

h 'We already have too much homework for tonight!'

.... the class.

i The students .... , 'Please, please,

please can we play a game?'

j 'It's a mouse!' .... the boy, jumping

onto a chair.

4 Change the words below into the parts of speech required. Take care with spelling.

fly – noun: .... flight ....

winter – adjective: ....

relax – noun: ....

live – adverb: ....

fear – adjective: ....

terror – verb: ....

luck – adverb: ....

open – noun: ....

relief – verb: ....

probably – noun: ....

explain – noun: ....

rely – adjective: ....

deny – noun: ....

relate – noun: ....

practice – verb: ....

prefer – adverb: ....

option – verb: ....

similar – noun: ....

ready – adverb: ....

peace – adjective: ....

assemble – noun: ....

5 Use your own words to complete the five sentences below after the dash. Use phrases that are unexpected, dramatic or an afterthought.

He went for a bike ride – but returned without the bike. ....

a They did not intend it to happen – ....

....

b It had been planned very carefully – ....

....

c A horrific scene awaited them – ....

....

d They ate supper, watched television, went to bed – ....

....

e I think it would be a good idea actually – ....

....

6 **Turn the following pairs of sentences into one compound sentence by joining them with either 'and', 'but', 'so' or 'or'.**

They were late for school. They started to run.

They were late for school, so they started to run.

a Their teacher was absent. They had to do the test anyway.

....

b He visited the zoo on his birthday. He had a party.

....

c 'There are no more copies of the book. You will have to share one between two.'

....

d Children should be polite to their elderly relatives. They should not look bored.

....

e The lion ate most of Jim. It didn't eat his head.

....

f We can go in that shop if you like. I don't think you'll find what you need.

....

g It's getting quite late. I think you should go home now.

....

h He has worked hard in class. He has done well in his exams.

....

i You can go there on foot if you like. You can also go there by bus, which will be much quicker.

....

j The time has come. It is important to recognise it.

....

7 **Turn the following pairs of sentences into one sentence by changing the first or second verb into a present participle (ending in 'ing'). A comma must be used between the two clauses.**

She arrived home. She realised she had forgotten to take her key.

Arriving home, she realised she had forgotten to take her key.

a The team played well. The team scored five goals.

....

b He sat on a bench in the garden. He ate his breakfast.

....

c Their grandmother set out for the market. She carried a basket.

....

d We walked to school together. We didn't talk at all.

....

e They hoped to find the place before dark. They continued their journey.

....

8 **The mini-saga below is too long. Reduce it to exactly 50 words, without losing any meaning, and then copy it out. Pay attention to punctuation.**

Race against time

The clock was ticking loudly now, and his heart started racing. Would he be able to do it quickly enough? His whole future depended on not running out of time. There wouldn't be a second chance to get it right. He'd prepared himself for a long time, and it was now or never. He was sweating now, and his hand was shaking. Too late. The invigilator called, 'Put your pens down now.' (72 words)

....

....

....

....

....

....

....

....

....

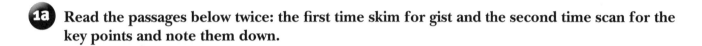

UNIT 3 Favourite things

This unit gives you practice in making notes for summary; building sentences; sequencing ideas; and using 'would' hypothetically. There are also exercises on using images and adjectives, and thinking about their order.

1a Read the passages below twice: the first time skim for gist and the second time scan for the key points and note them down.

On 1st April 1957 there was a mixed reaction to a BBC spoof documentary about spaghetti crops in Switzerland.

The presenter of the hoax *Panorama* programme was Richard Dimbleby, a distinguished broadcaster. The programme showed a family from Ticino in Switzerland carrying out their annual spaghetti harvest.

The women were carefully plucking strands of spaghetti from a tree and laying them in the sun to dry.

However, some viewers failed to see the funny side of the broadcast and criticised the BBC for including the item on a serious factual programme.

Other people were so intrigued that they asked where they could purchase their own spaghetti bush.

Spaghetti was not a widely eaten food in the UK in 1957 and many people thought it was an exotic delicacy.

Mr Dimbleby commented that each year the end of March is a very anxious time for spaghetti harvesters all over Europe because severe frost can impair the flavour of the spaghetti.

The programme explained how each strand of spaghetti always grows to exactly the same length, thanks to years of hard work by generations of growers.

This is believed to have been one of the first times television was used to stage an April Fools' Day hoax.

When viewers rang the BBC to ask how they could acquire a spaghetti tree, they were advised to plant a strand of spaghetti in a tin of tomato sauce and wait patiently for results.

....

....

....

....

....

....

....

....

....

The 'left-handed burger'

1998: A well-known fast-food chain published a full-page advertisement in *USA Today* announcing the introduction of a new item to their menu: a 'Left-handed veggie burger especially designed for the 32 million left-handed Americans'. According to the advertisement, the new burger included the same ingredients as the original burger, but all the contents were rotated 180 degrees for the benefit of their left-handed customers.

The following day the restaurant issued a follow-up release revealing that although the 'left-handed veggie burger' was a hoax, thousands of customers had gone into restaurants to request the new sandwich. Furthermore, according to the press release, 'many others requested their own "right-handed" version'.

Left-handed Veggie Burger

....

....

....

....

....

1b Using the notes you made for each of the passages above, write one sentence to describe each of the April Fool food hoaxes.

Spaghetti harvest

....

....

....

....

Left-handed burger

....

....

....

....

2 Look again at the passage on the spaghetti harvest. The information could be arranged in a more logical sequence. Put numbers next to each paragraph to show how the structure could be improved.

3 As an April Fool hoax, a supermarket announced that it had a new fruit in stock, the pinana, i.e. a combination of a pineapple and a banana. Write an advertisement for this new fruit, using lots of adjectives.

....

....

....

....

....

....

4 Using the language of restaurant menus, which has several adjectives in front of each noun, describe your favourite pizza and topping. Try to use some compound adjectives (those containing a hyphen), for example 'honey-roasted'.

....

....

....

....

....

....

....

....

5 Join the five sentences below using 'and', 'but' or 'so' to make one sentence, removing or replacing unnecessary words.

a It was my birthday.

b We went out for a meal.

c The meal was delicious.

d The restaurant was crowded.

e The restaurant was very noisy.

....

....

....

....

....

....

6a Use a dictionary or a thesaurus and work with a partner to rank the five adjectives in the lists below in order of strength of meaning: 1 is the lowest and 5 is the highest. Put a number above each adjective.

a bright, dazzling, shimmering, shining, gleaming

b dull, dowdy, dark, shady, shadowy

c sweet-smelling, perfumed, fragrant, scented, aromatic

d attractive, beautiful, pretty, stunning, magnificent

e funny, hilarious, amusing, humorous, comic

6b Write five sentences, each containing one of the five adjectives which scored 5 in the previous exercise, to show its strength of meaning.

a ....

....

b ....

....

c ....

....

d ....

....

e ....

....

7 Rearrange these lists of adjectives into the usual order for placing multiple adjectives before a noun (size, shape, age, colour, substance), for example 'a big, round, old, pink, fluffy rug', and use them in a sentence in front of a suitable noun.

a black, huge, hairy

....

....

b metal, square, old-fashioned

....

....

c Italian, wooden, long

....

....

d green, slimy, enormous

....

....

e knitted, rectangular, striped

....

....

8 **Put the verb in the right tense in the five sentences below. They describe things that have not happened but could (in theory) happen.**

a If I ruled the world, every day .... (be) the first day of spring.

b If she managed to arrive on time at the restaurant, it ....
(mean) that we could eat earlier.

c You .... (not find) much to eat at a Japanese restaurant if
you don't like fish.

d This paint colour does not match the new carpet so it ....
(be) better to choose another one.

e Can you tell me how much it .... (cost) if we bought a
return ticket?

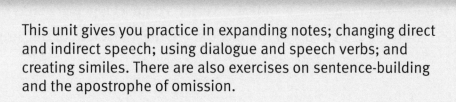

UNIT 4 School stories

This unit gives you practice in expanding notes; changing direct and indirect speech; using dialogue and speech verbs; and creating similes. There are also exercises on sentence-building and the apostrophe of omission.

1 **Expand the following notes into a paragraph.**

started school aged 5; very small; in our village; walked to school; aged 11 changed to private secondary school in town; travel by bus; especially enjoy team sports and English; big differences in class sizes and facilities; more friends; also more homework; Mrs Jackson kindest teacher because smiles a lot; find maths a difficult subject; maths teacher strict but maths has improved

....

....

....

....

....

....

....

2 Change the following sentences from indirect/reported to direct speech. Don't forget you may have to add other punctuation as well as inverted commas (speech marks).

a The teacher asked the class if any of them could tell her the name of the author.

....

....

b Sarah told her brother that she hadn't understood that day's English lesson.

....

....

c He asked her if she wanted him to help her with her homework.

....

....

d They admitted that they had forgotten what they had learned the week before and wouldn't be able to do the test.

....

....

e The teacher told the class that they couldn't leave the room until the bell had rung.

....

....

3 Change the following sentences from direct to indirect/reported speech. Don't forget you may have to remove other punctuation as well as the inverted commas (speech marks).

a The teacher said to me, 'Do your homework again and give it in tomorrow.'

....

....

b   He asked his neighbour, 'Will you lend me your book?'

....

....

c   'Did you understand what we have to do?' asked my partner.

....

....

d   'We can't do the test this lesson because we aren't prepared,' the students told the teacher.

....

....

e   'Stephano, leave the room immediately and report to the principal!' ordered the teacher.

....

....

4   **Turn the following script into a dialogue. Remove the names at the beginning and add inverted commas (speech marks) and a variety of speech verbs to show who is speaking and in what way, either before or after the speech.**

Student: Have you got time to help me with a problem?

'Have you got time to help me with a problem?' asked the student.
....

Student: I don't understand how to punctuate dialogue. Can you tell me again please?

Teacher: The first thing to remember is that when the speaker changes, you have to show this by starting a new line, the same as when you start a new paragraph.

Student: I understand that part. What I don't get is what you have to put at the end of each of the speeches in the conversation.

Teacher: You put a full stop – if it's not a question or exclamation – unless you are going on to say 'he said' or something like that. Then you put a comma instead of the full stop.

Student: And what about before starting the speech, and inside the speech?

Teacher: If the sentence has already begun, then you put a comma before opening the inverted commas. The punctuation inside the speech is the same as for any writing.

Student: Thanks a lot. I think I can do my homework now.

....

....

....

....

....

....

....

....

....

....

....

5 Direct speech can be introduced at the beginning, split in the middle, or finished off with a speech verb at the end. Use all three ways for the speeches below, being careful with the punctuation. Add a suitable person and speech verb, avoiding 'said'. For example:

Her father insisted, 'I have no idea whether he will be coming or not.'

'I have no idea,' her father insisted, 'whether he will be coming or not.'

'I have no idea whether he will be coming or not,' her father insisted.

a 'I've had enough so I'm going home!'

....

....

b 'Don't you dare bring that into the classroom again!'

....

....

....

c 'We're really sorry, and we won't forget next time.'

....

....

....

d 'Now, class, I'd like you to open your book at page 106.'

....

....

....

e 'Please can you give me a homework extension, because I was ill yesterday?'

....

....

....

6 **Write out the text below in a mixture of direct and indirect/reported speech, replacing 'said' in each case with a more precise verb, for example 'explained'.**

My brother said he wouldn't help me with my homework because he hated doing homework and had enough trouble with his own. He said that he didn't think that my helping him to learn his French verbs for a test was the same thing. He said that in any case he couldn't help me with English because he was no good at English and had just got a really bad grade for his latest composition. He said that it was because he hadn't punctuated the direct speech properly.

....

....

....

....

....

....

....

....

....

7 **Suggest appropriate and original ways of completing the following descriptions with similes to describe character.**

Her eyes twinkled like *jewels in sunlight.*

a The old woman's face in the picture was as wrinkled as

....

b The boy was running so fast away from the school gates, it was as if

....

c Everything about her appearance gave the impression of

....

d The welcoming smile of his new teacher was like

....

e On the day of the exam, he was as nervous as

....

8 Rewrite the simple sentences below as a paragraph, joining the sentences with either 'and', 'so', 'but' or 'or' to make three compound sentences.

   a It was breaktime.

   b The class was let out into the playground.

   c It was raining.

   d They could play in the covered area.

   e They could go to the hall.

   f They were not allowed to get wet.

   g Some children wanted to play in the rain.

   h They stayed outside.

   i Their clothes got soaked.

   j They were sent home.

....

....

....

....

....

....

....

....

....

....

9 Write out the words below in full, replacing the apostrophe with the missing letters. Be careful because there are some irregularities.

   a they're ....

   b 'til ....

   c you've ....

   d it's ....

   e o'clock ....

   f she'd ....

g don't ....

h can't ....

i could've ....

j won't ....

10 Contract the words and phrases below, using apostrophes to replace the removed letters. Be careful because there are some irregularities.

a would have ....

b he has ....

c I am not ....

d you had ....

e you would ....

f did not ....

g shall not ....

h should have ....

i must not ....

UNIT 5 Up in the air

This unit gives you practice in selecting points, paraphrasing, sequencing, and sentence-building for summary writing. There are also exercises on vocabulary choices and where to put full stops and commas.

1 **List six sub-headings to summarise the content of the six paragraphs below about the history of aviation.**

Aeroplanes were once made of cotton, metal and wood, but many things have changed since then. Aeroplanes improved once military and army work was found for them, which really began in 1914. The aircraft improved in structure because the plane had to be able to carry heavy weapons.

During the 1930s and the Second World War it was possible for planes to be bigger and to fly faster, farther and higher, as well as to carry heavier loads. Advances in aerodynamics helped engineers design ways to cut through the air smoothly.

As planes flew higher, pilots and passengers had increased difficulty breathing in the thin air at high altitudes, so pressurised cabins were invented, which made breathing easier at 30,000 feet. In addition, improved radio equipment allowed pilots to receive flight directions from the ground. Automatic pilots also came into use during the 1930s. These devices made more accurate navigation possible and helped pilots avoid becoming tired on long flights.

All the major advances in aeroplane designs in the 1930s went into building the Douglas DC-3. This twin-engine transport plane made its first passenger flights in 1936. It could accommodate 21 passengers and could fly smoothly at 170 mph. It soon became the main transport plane of the world's major airlines.

In 1958, Pan America World Airway began the first regular jet service between New York City and Paris using the American Boeing 707 jet. This was a popular airline, which made it possible for people other than the military to travel by air.

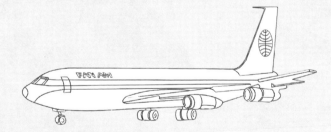

Aircraft have improved many times over the years, but engineers are working to design even bigger and better planes for the future, which will offer greater passenger comfort and reduce air pollution.

1 ....

2 ....

3 ....

4 ....

5 ....

6 ....

2 **Select the summary points about tornadoes in the following passage by underlining them. Using your own words, list the summary points on page 31.**

A tornado is a powerful, rotating column of air extending from a thunderstorm to the ground. The most violent tornadoes are capable of tremendous destruction, with wind speeds of up to 300 mph. They can flatten large buildings, uproot trees and hurl vehicles hundreds of metres. Damage-paths can be up to 2 km wide and 80 km long. In an average year, 1000 tornadoes are reported in the USA alone.

In extreme weather, emergencies can occur at any time, so you need survival food for such situations. By taking special precautions and keeping extra supplies, you'll be more likely to stay safe.

Most tornadoes form from thunderstorms. They need warm, moist air and cool, dry air. When these two air masses meet, they cause instability in the atmosphere. A change in wind direction and an increase in wind speed and height creates an invisible, horizontal spinning effect in the lower atmosphere. Rising air within the updraft tilts the rotating air from horizontal to vertical. An area of rotation, between 3 and 9 km wide, now extends through much of the storm and creates strong and violent tornadoes from within.

It is not fully understood how exactly tornadoes form, grow and die. Tornado researchers are still trying to solve the tornado puzzle, but for every piece that seems to fit they often uncover new pieces that need to be studied.

List your summary points about tornadoes here.

....

....

....

....

....

....

....

3 **Change the following phrases from the passage in exercise 2 into your own words, as far as possible:**

a powerful, rotating column of air

....

b capable of tremendous destruction

....

c taking special precautions

....

d cause instability in the atmosphere

....

e solve the tornado puzzle

....

4 Go back to your list in exercise 2 and give each one a number to show the order in which you think it would be logical to use and link the information.

5 Now use your list to write a summary of tornadoes. Where possible, join your points into compound sentences and sentences using present participles (i.e. 'ing' verb forms).

....

....

....

....

....

....

....

....

6 Reduce the passage below and on page 33 about hang-gliding to three sentences. The sentences should contain all the key information to answer this question: 'What do you need to know if you want to become a hang-glider pilot?'

Hang-gliding has developed since the 1970s into a practical and relatively safe sport, using a simple yet sophisticated machine built of aluminium, carbon-fibre and high-tech sail fabrics. Hang-glider pilots, suspended from their gliders by a special harness, launch from hills facing into the wind or are towed aloft from an airfield behind a microlight aircraft. The objective is to stay airborne using air currents for as long as possible. The UK record for distance currently stands at over 250 km, and for altitude at 5 000 metres.

A top-of-the range competition hang-glider can cost more than $7 000 new but second-hand ones are much less. A full training course will cost around $1 500, though a shorter introductory course is less expensive. It normally takes about ten days to train, plus some theory lessons in the classroom, and then you take a test. Pilots also need a harness, helmet, flying suit and boots; additional bits of equipment, such as instruments, may be required as you progress.

The pilot launches his or her machine by running to accelerate it to flying speed, then relaxes into the comfortable harness while controlling the glider by moving their weight in relation to the control bar. Competitions are held at club, national and international level.

Setting off on a sunny day on a long cross-country flight over attractive scenery, using only the natural power of the atmosphere and your own skill, gives a hang-glider pilot an exhilarating feeling of achievement.

....

....

....

....

....

....

....

....

....

7 Put pairs of commas in the passage below to show which parts of the sentence are 'removable' (i.e. which bits are not part of the essential grammatical structure).

He wanted, more than anything in the world, to be able to fly fast.

It wasn't long before Jonathan Gull was off by himself again far out at sea hungry happy learning.

The subject was speed and in a week's practice he learned more about speed than the fastest gull alive.

From a thousand feet flapping his wings as hard as he could he pushed over into a blazing steep dive toward the waves and learned why seagulls don't make blazing steep power-dives. In just six seconds he was moving seventy miles per hour the speed at which one's wing goes unstable on the upstroke.

Time after time it happened. Careful as he was working at the very peak of his ability he lost control at high speed.

From Jonathan Livingston Seagull *by Richard Bach*

8 Put full stops, capital letters and commas in the passage about lightning.

There are many kinds of lightning which is a flash of bright light produced by natural electricity it is one of nature's deadliest and most unpredictable phenomena typically occurring during thunderstorms when it is accompanied by thunder the lightning seems to happen before the thunder but this is not really true because the sound of the thunder takes longer to reach our ears than it takes our eyes to see the flash lightning can travel at up to 220,000 km/hr it is also very hot sometimes reaching a

temperature of 30,000 degrees centigrade there are about 16 million lightning storms in the world each year it can be caused by violent forest fires or ash clouds from volcanic eruptions the most common kinds of lightning are cloud to ground and intra cloud whereas sheet and forked lightning are quite rare the place that experiences the most lightning strikes is Florida USA.

9 Re-order the facts about lightning more logically in a numbered list below.

....

....

....

....

....

....

10 Use a dictionary or a thesaurus to rank the five words in the lists below in order of strength of meaning: 1 is the lowest and 5 is the highest. Put a number above each word.

a **cold**: icy, freezing, chilly, cool, bitter

b **hot**: blistering, baking, burning, boiling, scorching

c **wind**: breezy, gale-force, blustery, draughty, gusty

d **rain**: torrential, spitting, drizzling, downpour, cloudburst

e **fog**: misty, hazy, dense, unclear, thick

11 Write five sentences, each containing one of the five words you gave a score of 5 to in the previous exercise, to show their strength of meaning.

a ....

....

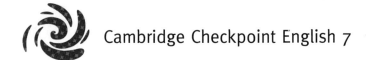

b ....

....

c ....

....

d ....

....

e ....

....

12 **Summarise the meaning or message of the poem below in two sentences, one for each verse, without using any of the words in the poem. You may change the order of the ideas.**

The Eagle
He clasps the crag with crooked hands;
Close to the sun in lonely lands,
Ringed with the azure world, he stands.

The wrinkled sea beneath him crawls;
He watches from his mountain walls,
And like a thunderbolt he falls.

Alfred Lord Tennyson

Eagles..

....

....

....

....

UNIT 6 Imaginary worlds

This unit gives you practice in forming relative ('who' and 'which') clauses; using past tenses; summarising; forming comparisons; and using specific descriptive words. There is also a reminder of irregular plurals and simple words that are easily confused.

1 Use 'who', 'which' or 'whose' to join together the simple sentences below. Put the joining words as close as possible to the words they are referring to, and put commas before them.

The spaceship was shaped like a saucer. It gave out a flickering, greenish light.

The spaceship, which was shaped like a saucer, gave out a flickering, greenish light.

a The strange noises frightened the children. The children decided to leave the house. The house also had an unpleasant smell.

....

....

b 'I'd like you to meet Sherlock Holmes. Mr Holmes is a famous detective.'

....

....

c The owner of the house was away. His wife had been in hospital recently.

....

....

d She said she had not noticed the alien. The alien had been following her for several hours.

....

....

....

e There was light coming from under the attic door. The door was locked.

....

....

2 **Reduce the plot outline of the gothic fantasy novella *Boy in Darkness* to no more than 50 words.**

> This story features Titus Groan, a character who also appears in Mervyn Peake's three novels set in the remote earldom of Gormenghast. In the novella, the 14-year-old hero longs for freedom from his senseless, rigid and never-ending duties in the ancient castle which he will inherit as the 77th Earl of Gormenghast. He escapes through a maze and encounters for the first time the nightmare world outside the castle, where in a grey, dream-like adventure he wanders through a bleak landscape, and then is driven by hunger and exhaustion into the underground tunnels of a disused mine. He is captured by the wicked Goat and Hyena, the followers of an evil emperor called Lamb who seeks to enslave him, which would make his new life even more of an imprisonment than the one he has escaped from.

....

....

....

....

....

....

....

....

3 Put the verbs in the sentences below into the correct past tense. Think carefully about the order in which the actions and events take place (e.g. I *had seen* the mysterious object in the garden *before* I *went* outside).

a We .... (decide) at our meeting that when we

.... (arrive) we ....

(hide) and wait to see what .... (happen).

b When our neighbour .... (return)

home, she .... (not notice) our ball,

which .... (lie) in her garden, where

we .... (throw) it by accident while we

.... (play) basketball.

c At the edge of the forest we .... (discover) a cave,

which we .... (not see) previously because we

.... (never go) that far.

d While he .... (explore) inside the dark and dusty room,

he .... (find) a box with carvings on its lid, which

.... (make) many centuries before.

e When I .... (wake up),

I .... (lie) on

the floor, and I could not remember

what .... (happen).

4 **Give the irregular plural form of the following nouns.**

a sheep ....

b knife ....

c goose ....

d fish ....

e wolf ....

f lady ....

g woman ....

h person ....

i party ....

j delay ....

5 **The list below shows 15 words that are often confused. Write a sentence for each word that shows you know its meaning.**

a where	**d** there	**g** theirs	**j** to	**m** who's
b were	**e** their	**h** there's	**k** two	**n** your
c we're	**f** they're	**i** too	**l** whose	**o** you're

a ....

b ....

c ....

d ....

e ....

f ....

g ....

h ....

i ....

j ....

k ....

l ....

m ....

n ....

o ....

6 **Put capital letters where necessary in the sentences below.**

a We thought the art exhibition in the national gallery in beijing was very interesting, and i bought a poster of a sculpture by ai weiwei called template.

b 'This is so boring! Can we go to the cinema instead? There's a good film on about samurai warriors called seven swords.'

c She has seven uncles; her favourite is uncle mark, and she enjoys going shopping with his wife, her aunt patience, and her cousin, matilda.

d The red fort in old delhi in northern india, which was built by the great mughal emperor shah jahan, is also called lal qila.

e In north america and canada, many rivers feed into the great lakes on the canadian border with the united states, including the river niagara, which leads to the falls.

7 **Circle the 15 errors in this piece of writing, and then write the corrections on page 42.**

One day, me and my best friend, Kim, decided to go to the place were their was an old house we could explore. When we got there, we heard a strange noise coming from inside, and it sounded like someone was crying in pain. We went cautiously through the open front door, hoping not to come across any rats or mouses. The noise got louder and we could tell it was coming from the cellar.

'I don't want to go any further,' I said. 'This is as something in a horror movie.'

'Your always scared of everything,' said my friend. 'Theirs no one here. It's just the wind.'

We went to the door of the cellar and listened. Then my friend called out bravely, Whose they're?' At first we could here only the leafs rustling against the downstairs windows, but suddenly me and Kim got a big surprise when the screaming began again, much nearer this time.

Kim turned as pale like a piece of paper, and said, 'You're right! I'm not staying here any longer. Who knows what's down their?' And then I was on my own.

a ....   i ....

b ....   j ....

c ....   k ....

d ....   l ....

e ....   m ....

f ....   n ....

g ....   o ....

h ....

8 **Replace the words in bold in the sentences below with words that are more descriptive.**

  a Two years before, the family had moved into a **nice** house in the countryside.

  ....

  b She became fascinated by the **big** picture hanging over the fireplace.

  ....

  c A **small** creature was scurrying across the path.

  ....

  d 'Since your behaviour has been so **bad**, you must be locked in your room.'

  ....

  e She was a **good** student, unlike the rest of the gang.

  ....

UNIT 7 Down to earth

This unit gives you practice in using apostrophes, commas and prepositions. You will also look at movement verbs, onomatopoeia and similes.

1 **Replace the gaps in the sentences with either 'its' or 'it's', depending on whether it shows possession (no apostrophe) or has missing letters (with apostrophe).**

a I think .... time to go, as .... already later than

we agreed.

b I like my garden with .... lawn and tall shady trees.

.... where I spend most of my time.

c 'Do you think .... a good

idea to let the canary out of

.... cage?' my mother asked.

d '..................................... alright,' I answered.

'..................................... not likely to fly very far,

as .... never been out of

this room.'

e .... proverbial that a dog's bark is much worse than

.... bite.

2 **Put commas in the passage to separate items in a list or clauses in a sentence, or to show the parts of a sentence that could be removed.**

The tortoise is a land-dwelling reptile closely related to the tortoise's marine cousin the sea turtle. The tortoise is found in many countries around the world but particularly in the southern hemisphere where the weather is warmer for most of the year.

Tortoises have a hard outer shell to protect them from predators but the skin on the legs head and belly of the tortoise is quite soft so the tortoise is able to retract its limbs into its shell to protect itself. The tortoise's shell can range in size from a few centimetres to a couple of metres depending on the species.

Most species of tortoise have a herbivorous diet eating grasses weeds flowers leafy greens and fruits. Tortoises generally have a lifespan similar to that of humans although some species of tortoise like the giant tortoise have been known to reach over 150 years old.

There are many different species of tortoise around the world and they vary in size colour and diet. Most species of tortoise are active during the day but in places with hot climates tortoises will often venture out to find food at the cooler times of dawn and dusk.

3 **Complete the sentences below with either 'as', 'as if' or 'like'.**

a 'I don't know if it is the same creature we saw earlier, but it certainly looks

.... it.'

b The ancient building looked .... it had been built in the medieval

period.

c The goat and the hyena looked .... creatures from a nightmare,

and were as frightening .... one's worst fears.

d 'Do exactly .... I have told you,' said the witch. 'If you disobey,

you will end up .... your brother.'

e They followed meekly, ... lambs, afraid that they might be changed

into something, ... their friend had been.

4a **Fill in the blanks with appropriate prepositions, like 'in' or 'at'. Some may need more than one.**

a She was interested .... biology and looked forward

.... the day when she could study the subject ....

university and then take it .... as a career.

b They were not aware .... the fact that something was hiding

.... the corner .... the end ....

the corridor, and that it was about to creep .... them.

c The man was wanted .... the police .... a crime

which had been committed .... the early hours ....

the morning .... the neighbouring district.

d 'I don't see what there is to complain .... ,' said the shopkeeper

.... a frown. 'The bike is .... the sale, so you

can have it .... a reduced price, and if you are not satisfied

.... it, you can return it and have your money ....

e They found the missing tortoise................................... the side ....

the road, where it had been all along; it had apparently set ....

to return .... the place it had come .... the

first place.

4b **Circle the correct preposition in the paired sentences.**

a There's no room here; put it **at** / **in** the end.

   Did you manage to get there **at** / **in** the end?

b It's important to get to your lessons **on** / **in** time.

   I don't think we are going to arrive at the station **on** / **in** time to say goodbye.

c The shop you are looking for is **on** / **in** the corner of the street.

   There was a lot of junk piled up **on** / **in** the corner of the room.

d The man was last seen walking quickly **along** / **in** the street.

   You shouldn't throw litter **along** / **in** the street.

e During the match he was hit **on** / **in** the head.

   There was a fear that he had been wounded **on** / **in** the head.

f The table was made **of** / **from** two old crates.

   The table was made **of** / **from** the best mahogany.

g It was surprising to see how many people got **off** / **out of** the car.

   As the vehicle had broken down, all the passengers got **off** / **out of** the bus.

h Before long, they arrived **at** / **in** their grandmother's house.

   They arrived **at** / **in** Tokyo just before dawn.

i I don't think much **of** / **about** the new headteacher.

   You need to think more **of** / **about** your use of prepositions.

j The old bicycle is not **in** / **on** good condition.

   I will lend it to you **in** / **on** one condition.

5 Put each of these verbs of movement in a sentence that shows its meaning. You may need to check in a dictionary first.

a amble

....

....

b whirl

....

....

c tiptoe

....

....

d dodge

....

....

e saunter

....

....

f shuffle

....

....

g scuttle

....

....

h slither

....

....

i writhe

....

....

j skip

....

....

6a **Which onomatopoeic words would you use to describe the following sounds?**

a the barking of a dog ....

b the noise of wind ....

c the sound of flames ....

d the exploding of a bomb ....

e the breaking of a window ....

f the bursting of a balloon ....

g a collision between cars ....

h the sound made by cicadas ....

i a boat engine ....

j a drill ....

6b What do the following onomatopoeic sounds remind you of?

a whistling...

b rustling..

c clattering...

d chattering..

e pattering..

7 Complete the images with your own comparisons.

a The buzzing of the flies was very annoying and reminded her of......................................

....

b The body of the beetle was as green and shiny as...

....

c The mice in the cage were greyish-brown, the colour of..

....

d The scorpion's tale was curved, the same shape as...

....

e The shell of the tortoise felt like..

....

UNIT 8 Hidden treasure

This unit gives you practice in using active and passive verbs, commas, and relative clauses. You will also look at negative prefixes, adverb endings and the apostrophe of possession.

1 Add the correct negative prefix – 'un', 'in', 'dis' or 'mis' – to the words below, and then use each new word in a sentence that explains its meaning. There may be more than one possible new word.

a understand: ....

....

....

b like: ....

....

....

c fit: ....

....

....

d count: ....

....

....

e sufficient: ....

....

....

2 Give a synonym or paraphrase for these words with negative prefixes, using the same part of speech.

a dissimilar ....

b unsatisfactory ....

c dissuade ....

d mistake ....

e immature ....

f irregular ....

g unappealing ....

h disadvantage ....

i misled ....

j unfit ....

3 Insert the correct word – who, which, whom or whose – in the gaps in the following sentences.

a I have no idea .... you are talking about, or ....

day you are referring to.

b .... money is this lying on the floor? Does it belong to the girl

.... was here earlier?

c They reached the cave, ... was marked on the map, but they

couldn't find the person .... was supposed to be meeting them there.

d We were frightened by the strange-looking animal .... was standing

in the middle of the road, ... howl sounded like a wolf's.

e '.. do you wish to speak to?' the receptionist asked.

'The person .... is responsible for arranging the trip,' the caller

answered.

4 **Change the verbs in the sentences below from active to passive form. You will need to use 'by' in most of them, to say who is performing the action, and make some other minor changes.**

a Captain Billy Bones hires Jim to keep a look out.

....

....

....

b A group of pirates raid the inn in search of a chest.

....

....

....

....

....

c They find a ship and a crew, and set out on their voyage.

....

....

d Jim warns his comrades of the crew's conspiracy.

....

....

e Long John Silver captures Jim and threatens to kill him.

....

....

5 Change the adjectives to adverbs. The rule is to add 'ly', but be careful of irregular forms.

a immediate ....

b fast ....

c helpful ....

d strong ....

e public ....

6 Change the adverbs below to adjectives. The rule is to take away the 'ly', but be careful of irregular forms.

a hardly ....

b practically ....

c carefully ....

d continuously ....

e fifthly ....

7 Insert commas in the passage below where they are needed to separate clauses in a sentence or items in a list, or to show phrases that could be removed without changing the sense. Examples include adverb phrases near the beginning of sentences (e.g. *Not surprisingly,* they all wanted chocolate) and appositional phrases, which give extra information (e.g. Frodo wants to take Sam, *his friend*, with him).

The Lord of the Rings begins in the Shire when Frodo Baggins inherits the Ring from Bilbo his cousin and guardian. Both are unaware of its evil origin but Gandalf the Grey a wizard and old friend of Bilbo knows the Ring's history and advises Frodo to take it away from the Shire. Frodo leaves taking his gardener and friend Sam Gamgee and two cousins Merry and Pippin Took as companions. They nearly encounter the Ringwraiths while still in the Shire but shake off pursuit by cutting through the Old Forest where they are aided by Tom Bombadil on whom the Ring has no effect. After leaving the Forest they stop in the town of Bree where they meet a man named Aragorn who joins them as guide and protector. They leave Bree having narrowly escaped another attack by the Ringwraiths but the Ringwraiths follow them to the look-out hill of Weathertop and they wound Frodo with a cursed knife. Aragorn leads the hobbits toward the Elven refuge of Rivendell while Frodo's health becomes worse. At the Ford of Bruinen the Ringwraiths attack again but flood waters controlled by Elrond master of Rivendell rise up and overwhelm them saving the company.

8 Cross out the incorrect apostrophes in these sentences and insert them where they are needed.

a Oranges' and lemons' were being sold at a reduced price at the greengrocers'.

b Marcus' friends' arrived at the party's end instead of at it's beginning.

c My toes' hurt because of my three weeks' of walking in the mountains'.

d In two day's time I will have completed a month's work on my project.

e We can meet in two days' at the bus' stop outside the men's sports' club near the chemist's.

9 Insert apostrophes in the passage below where they are needed to show possession, i.e. that something belongs to someone.

Sam rescues Frodo from Cirith Ungol, and they journey through Mordor. The mental weight of the Rings evil influence weakens Frodo considerably as they near Mount Doom, but he is aided by Sams support. Meanwhile, in order to give Sam and Frodo a chance to cross Mordor safely, Aragorn leads his remaining soldiers to march on the Black Gate of Mordor. In the climactic battle the vastly outnumbered alliance of Gondor and Rohan fight desperately against Saurons armies, with the intention of diverting Saurons attention from Mount Doom. At the edge of the Cracks of Doom, Frodo is unable to resist the Ring, and claims it for himself. Gollum suddenly reappears, struggles with Frodo for the Ring and bites off Frodos finger, Ring and all. However, in doing so he falls into the fire, taking the Ring with him, and the One Ring is thus destroyed. At the moment of its destruction, Sauron perishes, his armies begin to retreat, his tower crumbles into dust, the Ringwraiths disintegration occurs, and the War of the Ring finally ends.

UNIT 9 Meet the family

This unit gives you practice in using difficult spellings, more punctuation and conditional sentences. There is also further practice in doing selective summaries.

1 Put 'ie' or 'ei' into the gaps in the following words. Remember the rule is *i* before *e*, except after *c*, when the sound you are making is double *ee*. Be careful of the two exceptions to the rule.

a rec.................ve

b n.................ghbour

c prot.................n

d w.................rd

e s.................ze

f th.................f

g ach.................ve

h perc.................ve

i rel.................f

j ch.................f

2 Put the appropriate punctuation at the end of each sentence: full stop, question mark or exclamation mark.

a Will you please come here quickly

b And then they did exactly the opposite

c I am not here to discuss the accident

d Tell me all about yourself

e I can't believe that you just said that

f How very unfortunate

g Well, what a surprise

h They suddenly heard an almighty crash

i Do you really think that such a thing is possible

j My family means everything to me

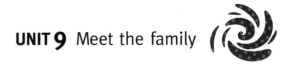

3 **Select and list the key points from the passage for a selective summary on the topic of the characters in the television show *The Simpsons*.**

The Simpson family is a family of fictional characters featured in the animated television series *The Simpsons*, which has been showing for more than twenty years in half-hour episodes. It began in the USA and is set in the town of Springfield. The inventor, the cartoonist Matt Groening, named the characters after members of his own family – except for Bart. Bart is an anagram of 'brat', and the character is based on Groening's elder brother, Mark.

The family consists of a married couple, Homer and Marge, and their three children: Bart, Lisa and baby Maggie. In addition to the five main family members, there are other characters who make frequent appearances. These are Homer's father, Marge's twin sisters, various neighbours and local shopkeepers, and staff of the elementary school.

Homer is a careless and clumsy character who has an inappropriate job as a safety inspector at a nuclear power station. His long-suffering, blue-haired wife always has to look after the children as he is unreliable and a bad role model. The only son, Bart, is ten years old and causes trouble wherever he goes – particularly at school. He is mischievous, sly, rebellious, and dislikes work of any kind. The eight-year-old Lisa is very different, being academically gifted and a saxophone player. Maggie, the least seen and heard member of the family, sucks a dummy and rarely speaks. The family live in a typical suburban house and have a dog and a cat.

The family are always having problems and falling out with each other, but they are a close-knit family really, and it is an extremely popular show with all age groups and nationalities. It has won many media awards. Homer's catch-phrase 'D'oh!' is recognised throughout the world and has even been included in dictionaries. Bart's catch-phrase of 'Eat my shorts' is equally well known.

....

....

....

....

....

....

....

....

....

....

....

4 **Put one or more hyphens in each sentence. You can remind yourself of how hyphens are used by looking at those used in the passage in exercise 3 about *The Simpsons*.**

   a The long haired teenager with a pony tail, a sixteen year old boy, was sometimes mistaken for a girl.

   b Your attitude may be grown up but it is rather old fashioned, and you are also badly dressed, so I don't think you are suitable for the job.

   c My step father met with the ex headteacher of my school to discuss my future subject choices.

   d The one ton hippo disappeared into the six metre deep river.

   e The mock exams were put off until a month later, but the end of term progress reports were still sent out to parents.

5 **Put a dash in the the sentences that you think should have one, replacing the comma. You can remind yourself of how single dashes are used by looking at those used in the passage in exercise 3 about *The Simpsons*.**

   a I wish Jessica wouldn't try to get into our bedroom, or even come into the house at all.

   b We didn't expect the whole family to arrive at once, especially not at two o'clock in the morning.

   c It isn't a matter of money, but a matter of time.

   d My grandfather spent three months in hospital, and then he was fully recovered.

   e On the whole it all worked out well, although not at all as we had planned.

6 **Put the verb in the right tense and form in the conditional sentences below. Note that there are some irregularities and you may need to use the passive form.**

a If I were you I [not go] .... back to that

place ever again.

b Water boils if it [heat] .... to 100 degrees

centigrade.

c I [come] .... to your party if I had received

the invitation in time.

d Unless we hear from you by tomorrow, we [have to]

.... cancel the booking.

e They [attend] .... the ceremony if they were able to.

f If he [give] .... a choice, he would prefer to study History rather

than Geography.

g We would have got here earlier if the ferry [have not] ....

been cancelled.

h Unless you stop messing about in class, you [fail] .... your

end-of-term test.

i Bart Simpson [be happy] .... if his school was closed down.

j If Homer [continue] .... to eat as many doughnuts, he would

have become even more overweight.

7 **Select and underline the phrases in the following passage that you would use as quotations to support the idea that the speaker is very fond of her brother.**

Try as I might, I could never catch up with my brother. And I certainly tried hard. He was seven years ahead of me, which meant seven years of knowledge, seven years of experience and seven years of growing that I had to do very quickly. Impossible, of course, but it didn't stop me trying to narrow the gap. I thought he was marvellous. He taught me all sorts of games and whenever I beat him I thought he had been kind and let me win. All I wanted was to be like him.

This worshipping reached a peak when I was ten. My brother was learning to drive. Being able to drive was the most grown-up thing imaginable to me. How I longed for my seventeenth birthday! On my eleventh I remember thinking: 'Only six more years to go.'

By this time, though, my brother was on the verge of leaving home. I shall never forget the day he went. He had always been there and now, suddenly, he was leaving the family. I went into his bedroom, sat on his bed and cried. I cried bitterly, feeling utterly alone and lost. I had spent eleven and a half years with constant company – someone to play with, someone to fall out with, someone I loved. Of course, he came home for holidays, but it was never quite the same.

From Family Talk *by Rex Harley*

8 **Use this list of selected facts to write a news bulletin.**
- A ten-year-old dog is a veteran sky-diver.
- He is a pug.
- He has been parachuting for nine years.
- He jumps from planes, in tandem with his owner.
- He is called Otis.
- His owner is called Will da Silva.
- He is attached to his owner's chest in a harness.
- He wears dog goggles – 'doggles'.
- He has just completed his 64th sky-dive.
- He puts his legs out like a bird when sky-diving.
- They sky-dive at the Lodi Parachute Center in Acampo, Los Angles.
- Otis has been living the life since he was a pup and has become part of the family.
- He loves sky-diving and gets very excited waiting for the green light at the plane door.
- People are coming from across America to jump with the four-legged daredevil.

Otis, the sky-diving dog,

UNIT 10 Mysteries and puzzles

This unit gives you practice in vocabulary building, spelling, and close reading. Solving the mystery in each case depends on paying close attention to words and the letters within them.

1 **Read the paragraph, then answer the question.**

This is an unusual paragraph. I'm curious how quickly you can find out what is so unusual about it. It looks so plain you would think nothing was wrong with it. In fact, nothing is wrong with it! It is unusual though. Study it, and think about it, but you still may not find anything odd. But if you work at it a bit, you might find out.

Why is this paragraph so unusual?

....

....

2a **Change the word 'cat' to the word 'kid', changing only one letter each time to make a new word. Try to achieve this in no more than five stages.**

....

....

....

2b **Change the word 'read' to the word 'sail', changing only one letter each time to make a new word. Try to achieve this in no more than six stages.**

....

....

....

3a **Read the riddle below. The question is at the end of the riddle.**

As I was going to St Ives,
I met a man with seven wives.
Each wife had seven sacks,
Each sack had seven cats,
Each cat had seven kits.
Kits, cats, sacks and wives,
How many were going to St Ives?

....

3b **Everything Mr Red owns is red, he lives in a red bungalow and his chairs are red, his tables are red. His ceiling, walls and floor are all red. All of his clothes are red, his shoes are red, even his carpet, television and phone are red.**

What colour are his stairs?

....

4 **How many Fs are there in this sentence?** ....

FINISHED FILES ARE THE RESULT OF
YEARS OF SCIENTIFIC STUDY
COMBINED WITH THE EXPERIENCE
OF YEARS

5 **This poem is a warning not to trust computer spellcheckers because of the existence of homonyms (words that sound the same but are spelt differently). Rewrite the poem, in the column next to it, with the correct spellings. Watch out for the punctuation too.**

Eye have a spelling chequer   ....

It came with my pea sea   ....

It plain lee marques four my revue   ....

Miss steaks eye can knot sea.   ....

Eye strike a quay and type a whirred   ....

And weight four it two say   ....

Weather eye am wrong oar write   ....

It shows me strait a weigh.   ....

As soon as a mist ache is maid   ....

It nose bee fore two long   ....

And eye can put the error rite   ....

Its rare lea ever wrong.   ....

Eye have run this poem threw it   ....

I'm shore your pleased two no   ....

Its letter perfect awl the weigh   ....

My chequer tolled me sew.   ....

Adapted from Candidate for a Pullet Surprise, *by Jerrod H. Zar*

6 **When you have corrected the spelling of the poem, list the words in it that contain the following sounds.**

a long 'a' [eɪ]

....

....

b long 'e' [iː]

....

....

c long 'i' [aɪ]

....

....

7 **Find as many words as you can of three, four and five letters that are used in the word**

EXCALIBUR

....

....

....

....

....

....

....

....

8 **Read the poem below. It is a famous nonsense poem.**

Jabberwocky

'Twas brillig, and the slithy toves
Did gyre and gimble in the wabe;
All mimsy were the borogoves,
And the mome raths outgrabe.

'Beware the Jabberwock, my son!
The jaws that bite, the claws that catch!
Beware the Jubjub bird, and shun
The frumious Bandersnatch!'

He took his vorpal sword in hand:
Long time the manxome foe he sought –
So rested he by the Tumtum tree,
And stood awhile in thought.

And, as in uffish thought he stood,
The Jabberwock, with eyes of flame,
Came whiffling through the tulgey wood,
And burbled as it came!

> One, two! One, two! And through and through
> The vorpal blade went snicker-snack!
> He left it dead, and with its head
> He went galumphing back.
>
> 'And, has thou slain the Jabberwock?
> Come to my arms, my beamish boy!
> O frabjous day! Callooh! Callay!'
> He chortled in his joy.
>
> 'Twas brillig, and the slithy toves
> Did gyre and gimble in the wabe;
> All mimsy were the borogoves,
> And the mome raths outgrabe.
>
> *Lewis Carroll*

a Infer the poem's meaning and summarise the story in no more than three sentences.

....

....

....

....

....

....

b Identify the nonsense words in the poem and list them in the left-hand column below.

....

....

....

....

....

....

....

....

....

....

....

c In the right-hand column above, suggest a replacement real word for each nonsense word in the left-hand column, that would fit into the context and into the metre. You will need to consider the part of speech and the number of syllables in your replacement words.

9 Solve the riddles below.

a In marble walls as white as milk,
Lined with a skin as soft as silk,
Within a fountain crystal-clear,
A golden apple doth appear.
No doors there are to this stronghold,
Yet thieves break in and steal the gold.

What is it?

....

b I am the beginning of sorrow, and the end of sickness. You cannot express happiness without me, yet I am in the midst of crosses. I am always in risk, yet never in danger. You may find me in the sun, but I am never out of darkness.

What am I?

....

10a What do the following words have in common: madam, eye, deed, level, radar?

....

10b Can you think of more words that are similar?

....

11 **Find the 12 words in the wordsearch that are to do with crime.**

F	U	T	S	M	R	V	I	C	T	I	M
J	I	P	O	F	O	R	E	N	S	I	C
Y	K	N	Q	D	B	T	L	W	C	N	R
A	B	H	G	O	V	D	I	S	E	L	I
J	U	A	T	E	X	M	R	V	N	U	M
I	R	W	E	V	R	K	Z	B	E	J	I
T	G	U	D	I	A	P	Q	R	M	V	N
G	L	E	S	D	Y	B	R	U	N	G	A
C	A	D	R	E	V	A	L	I	B	I	L
P	R	A	U	N	S	H	E	L	N	O	G
S	K	I	N	C	A	R	R	E	S	T	U
V	O	R	D	E	T	E	C	T	I	V	E

....

....

....

....

....

....

12 Write crossword puzzle clues (i.e. definitions) for the words you have found in the wordsearch in exercise 11.

1 ....

2 ....

3 ....

4 ....

5 ....

6 ....

7 ....

8 ....

9 ....

10 ....

11 ....

12 ....

UNIT 11 Looking back

This unit gives you practice in sentence structuring; punctuation; contractions; and spellings. It also looks at the use of 'would' for the repeated past, irregular past tense verbs, and the verb form used after initial negatives.

1 **The following are non-sentences. Rewrite them as sentences, i.e. give them a main verb and correct the grammar if necessary.**

a Never again.

....

b No big deal!

....

c Because I say so.

....

d Maybe, and maybe not.

....

e And so to bed.

....

2 **The sentences below describe repeated actions in the past. Rewrite them, using 'would'.**

a Every year, we went to the mountains for our holiday.

....

b I often said to my mother that I didn't feel like going to school.

....

c Whenever it rained, we stayed inside at breaktime.

....

d I never found out where he disappeared to during the PE lessons.

....

....

....

e I used to leave early in the morning and did not return until late in the afternoon.

....

....

....

3 Rewrite these sentences, beginning with the words in bold.

a We **never** went to the mountains for our annual holiday.

....

b I **rarely** said to my mother that I didn't feel like going to school.

....

c The teacher was not in the classroom, nor were any of the students. (**neither**)

....

d I **never** found out where he disappeared to during the PE lessons.

....

e There was **no** sign of their presence in the deserted house.

....

4 **Using three different colours, mark paragraph breaks (//), full stops and commas in the passage.**

This memory has been on my conscience for a long time one day at school we had to do an English punctuation test I hadn't listened to the lesson and had forgotten about the test so I wasn't prepared for it I didn't know where to put full stops and commas so I looked over at the paper of my neighbour in the next row she was a girl I didn't like at all and she was also very good at English so she always got top marks I copied where she put her punctuation marks the teacher collected the tests in and I forgot about it a few days later the teacher said that she was very shocked that there had been some cheating in the class she explained that two of the test papers she had marked were identical she said that if there is copying in an exam both the students get no marks so she had given both papers a zero we were given the tests back and my neighbour burst into tears she never found out which of the other students around her had copied from her I want to say sorry to her now.

5a **Add apostrophes in the sentences to show where there are missing letters.**

a Weve an appointment at six oclock and its already half past five.

b The firework display doesnt begin til after dark.

c You couldve done it later if youd wanted to.

d The films complete rubbish, so dont bother going to see it.

e Whats the reason for its late arrival?

5b **Rewrite the contracted phrases below in full.**

a What's happened? What's the problem?

....

b The match can't be postponed; it just wouldn't be possible.

....

c If you won't do it, then someone else has to.

....

d He would've scored a higher mark if he'd done more practice.

....

e They're doing one thing, we're doing another, and everybody who's coming is helping with what's to be done.

....

....

6 Tick ✓ as right or mark ✗ as wrong the following spellings, and where necessary write corrections next to the misspelt words.

a wieght   ....

b thieves   ....

c protien   ....

d counterfeit   ....

e deceive   ....

f beleif   ....

g reign   ....

h reciept   ....

i eight   ....

j mischeivous   ....

7a Change these verbs into the simple past tense.

a hurry ....

b weep ....

c teach ....

d learn ....

e run ....

f cut ....

g lead	....		**l** forget	....
h swim	....		**m** lie	....
i meet	....		**n** lay	....
j send	....		**o** pay	....
k mean	....		**p** beat	....

7b **Change these verbs into the present tense.**

a lay	....	**i** lit	....
b stole	....	**j** fitted	....
c felt	....	**k** ate	....
d swam	....	**l** made	....
e occurred	....	**m** married	....
f caught	....	**n** became	....
g sought	....	**o** knelt	....
h thought	....	**p** won	....

8 **Think of three different ways of joining these sentences to make one, changing the order and adding connectives. Don't forget the commas!**

- The past always seems better than the present.
- The sun is always shining in one's memories.
- Returning is always a disappointment.

....

....

....

....

....

UNIT 12 Secret lives

This unit gives you practice in the formation of comparative and superlative adjectives; punctuation of dialogue; and use of apostrophes. You will also practise changing direct to indirect (reported) speech.

1 Give the comparative form of these adjectives, e.g. 'brighter', 'more comfortable'. Some are irregular. Think about spelling.

a sinister ....

b pretty ....

c slippery ....

d awful ....

e red ....

f dangerous ....

g fast ....

h shy ....

i steady ....

j pale ....

2 Give the superlative form of these adjectives, e.g. 'brightest', 'most comfortable'. Some are irregular. Think about spelling.

a interesting ....

b big ....

c safe ....

d lovely ....

e fearful ....

f hungry ....

g powerful ....

h ill ....

i sad ....

j little ....

3 **Circle the adjectival forms in the list that are incorrect, and correct them alongside.**

a successfuller ....

b wetter ....

c driest ....

d littlest ....

e furiouser ....

f ablest ....

g liveliest ....

h tiredest ....

i willinger ....

j carelessest ....

4 **Put inverted commas (speech marks) and any other punctuation where necessary in these sentences.**

a I don't think, she whispered, that we should ever mention the subject again.

b As they approached the house they heard someone shout Help! Fire!

c You don't know, I suppose, how many people are going to be present?

d Can you imagine what is going to happen next? she asked hesitantly.

e He ventured to suggest I propose that we take a different route.

5 **Put apostrophes of omission and possession in this passage.**

The childrens things were all over the place in the classroom, and the girls and boys exercise books were mixed up, so when the end of school came at four oclock they couldnt go home until theyd sorted them out and put everything in its place in the room.

'Its as if its been hit by a hurricane,' said the teacher. 'Theres a days work here to put things back in their proper places. In three weeks well be having a school open day, so youd better get used to everyones possessions being kept in their lockers. I dont want your parents to think that theres no need for you to be tidy when youre at school. Now lets get on with it so youll be able to go home before it gets dark.'

6 **For each of the sentences below, change the direct speech to indirect (reported) speech.**

a 'Yes, please! I really like this kind of food,' my sister replied.

My sister replied that
....

....

b When I got home my mother asked me, 'What did you do at school today?'

....

....

c 'We mustn't come here any more,' my friend insisted, 'because something nasty may be living here.'

....

....

d They arrived late and tired, and were greeted by their host with the words, 'How was your journey?'

....

....

e 'How did I do in the test?' the student asked.

'Not very well, I'm afraid,' replied the teacher.

....

....

7 **For each of the sentences below, change the indirect (reported) speech to direct speech.**

a My father enquired about whether I had finished my homework and suggested that I should do so before I started to watch television.

'Have you finished...'
....

....

b The excited students shouted an invitation to the others to come and join them for the singing and dancing that evening.

....

....

c My mother wanted to know why I had decided to give up going to basketball training.

....

....

d The student asked the teacher how to improve her vocabulary and whether doing more reading would be a good idea.

....

....

e The passenger instructed the taxi driver to turn left and to stop outside the house at the end of the road.

....

....

8 **Put paragraph breaks (//) in the passage below to show where a new paragraph should begin, in order to indicate a change of speaker or return to narrative from speech.**

Alice didn't like being criticised, so she began asking questions. 'Aren't you sometimes frightened at being planted out here, with nobody to take care of you?'. 'There's the tree in the middle,' said the Rose: 'What else is it good for?' 'But what could it do, if any danger came?' Alice asked. 'It says "Bough-wough!"' cried a Daisy: 'That's why its branches are called boughs!' 'Didn't you know THAT?' cried another Daisy, and here they all began shouting together, till the air seemed quite full of little shrill voices. 'Silence, every one of you!' cried the Tiger-lily, waving itself passionately from side to side, and trembling with excitement. 'They know I can't get at them!' it panted, bending its quivering head towards Alice, 'or they wouldn't dare to do it!' 'Never mind!' Alice said in a soothing tone, and stooping down to the daisies, who were just beginning again, she whispered, 'If you don't hold your tongues, I'll pick you!'. There was silence in a moment, and several of the pink daisies turned white. 'That's right!' said the Tiger-lily. 'The daisies are worst of all. When one speaks, they all begin together, and it's enough to make one wither to hear the way they go on!' 'How is it you can all talk so nicely?' Alice said, hoping to get it into a better temper by a compliment. 'I've been in many gardens before, but none of the flowers could talk.' 'Put your hand down, and feel the ground,' said the Tiger-lily. 'Then you'll know why. 'Alice did so. 'It's very hard,' she said, 'but I don't see what that has to do with it.' 'In most gardens,' the Tiger-lily said, 'they make the beds too soft–so that the flowers are always asleep.' This sounded a very good reason, and Alice was quite pleased to know it. 'I never thought of that before!' she said.

Adapted from Through the looking glass *by Lewis Carroll*

9 **Fill the gaps in the sentences with either 'was' or 'were'.**

a He looked as if he .... going to dive into the swimming pool.

b I would think very carefully about doing that, if I .... you.

c When I .... very young, I .... scared of most insects.

d 'Let me know if you .... intending to come to the meeting.'

e Until I .... certain, I .... not able to make a decision.

10 Can you write an acrostic on the word **DREAMS? The idea is to use images and interesting vocabulary that relate to the idea of the word. For example, the beginning of the first line could be:**

D Daring adventures... or Dazzled by... ....

R ....

E ....

A ....

M ....

S ....

Acknowledgements

The authors and publishers acknowledge the following sources of copyright material and are grateful for the permissions granted. While every effort has been made, it has not always been possible to identify the sources of all the material used, or to trace all copyright holders. If any omissions are brought to our notice, we will be happy to include the appropriate acknowledgements on reprinting.

p. 6 from *The Story of My Life* by Helen Keller, copyright © 2012 by Helen Keller, used by permission of the American Foundation for the Blind Helen Keller Archives, all rights reserved; p. 34 from *Jonathan Livingston Seagull* by Richard Bach, used with kind permission of the author; p. 60 from *Family Talk* by Rex Harley, used with kind permission of the author; p. 63 spell checker poem adapted from *Candidate for a Pullet Surprise* by Jerrod H. Zar, 1992